Countries of the World

Vietnam

by Michael Dahl

Content Advisor
Pho, Ba Long
Founder, Past Secretary of the Board
Vietnam Foundation

Bridgestone Books
an imprint of Capstone Press

Bridgestone Books are published by Capstone Press
151 Good Counsel Drive, P.O. Box 669, Mankato, Minnesota 56002
http://www.capstone-press.com

Library of Congress Cataloging-in-Publication Data
Dahl, Michael S.
    Vietnam/by Michael Dahl.
    p. cm.--(Countries of the world)
    Includes bibliographical references and index.
    ISBN 1-56065-740-5
    1. Vietnam--Juvenile literature. I. Title. II. Series:
Countries of the world (Mankato, Minn.)
DS556.3.D33   1998
959.7--dc21

                    97-41867
                      CIP
                      AC

Editorial credits:
Editor, Christy Steele; cover design, Timothy Halldin; interior graphics, James Franklin;
    photo research, Michelle L. Norstad

Photo credits:
Peter Armenia, 10, 16, 18
John Cang, 5 (right), 14, 20
Capstone Press, 5 (left)
Thomas D. Parker, 12
Joe Smolian, cover
Brian A. Vikander, 6, 8

Table of Contents

Fast Facts

Name: Socialist Republic of Vietnam
Capital: Hanoi
Population: More than 73 million
Language: Vietnamese
Religions: Buddhist, Taoist

Size: 127,816 square miles
  (332,322 square kilometers)
*Vietnam is about the size of the U.S.
  state of Nevada.*
Crops: Rice, fruits, soybeans

Maps

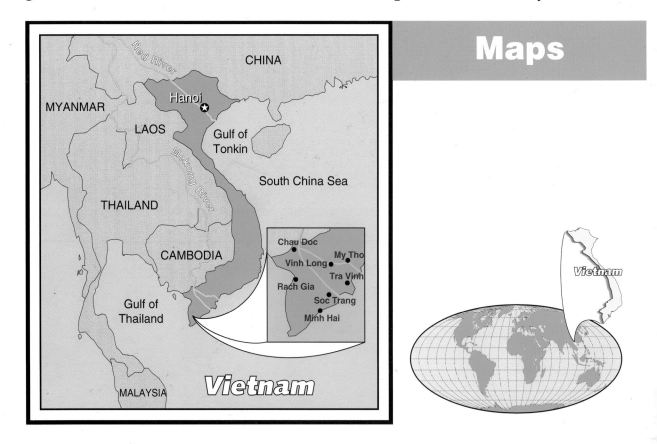

4

Flag

Vietnam's flag is red. Red stands for Communism. Communism is a way of ruling a country. Vietnam has a Communist government. The flag has a yellow star in the middle. The star stands for Vietnam.

Currency

The unit of currency in Vietnam is the dong.

About 10,000 dongs equal one U.S. dollar.

15,000   in 2004

The Land of Vietnam

Vietnam is a long, narrow country in southeast Asia. Vietnam lies south of China. The word Vietnam means far south. Vietnam's coast is 1,400 miles (2,254 kilometers) long. The middle of Vietnam is only 30 miles (48 kilometers) wide. The country curves like a giant letter S.

Much of Vietnam is covered with steep mountains. There are green jungles between the mountains. A jungle is land covered with trees, vines, and bushes.

Water forms Vietnam's eastern border. Vietnam touches the Gulf of Tonkin and the Gulf of Thailand. It also touches the South China Sea.

Vietnam was once divided into North Vietnam and South Vietnam. The countries fought a war against each other. North Vietnam won the war. Now, Vietnam is one country.

Water forms Vietnam's eastern border.

Rivers

Two major rivers flow through Vietnam. The Red River flows from China into the Gulf of Tonkin. People named it after the red soil that colors its waters. Hanoi sits on the banks of the Red River. Hanoi is the capital city of Vietnam.

The Mekong River is the longest river in Asia. It begins in the mountains of Tibet and flows 2,600 miles (4,160 kilometers). It ends in southern Vietnam.

The Mekong River turns into nine smaller rivers. These smaller rivers are called the Nine Dragons. The Nine Dragons create a delta. A delta is a wide, wet area. It is good for growing crops.

Many of Vietnam's people live in houses on the Mekong Delta. Some families live in boats on the rivers.

Many Vietnamese people are farmers. They plant rice in wet deltas. People all over the world buy Vietnamese rice.

Some Vietnamese farmers plant rice in wet deltas.

Going to School

Vietnamese children begin elementary school at age six. Students learn reading, writing, and math. They attend elementary school for seven years. Then they choose whether to enter secondary school or vocational school.

A vocational school offers classes to teach job skills. Students use these skills to work after they complete school.

Students who choose secondary schools receive a general education. They study history, science, math, music, and other subjects. The students must also study Russian or English. Most students prefer to learn English.

Many secondary school students attend college. College is a school people go to after secondary school. Vietnam has more than 100 colleges students can choose from.

Vietnamese students learn reading, writing, and math.

Vietnamese Food

Rice is the main food for people in Vietnam. Vietnamese people often add fish sauce to rice. The fish sauce is called nuoc mam (NOO-ahk MAHM). People sometimes add garlic, lemon, and sugar to nuoc mam.

Pho (FUH) is a popular food in Vietnam. Pho is soup made with thick rice noodles and beef. People usually have pho for breakfast.

Xoi (SOY) is another favorite dish. Xoi is sticky rice mixed with peanuts or beans. People wrap the mix in large leaves.

Many Vietnamese people enjoy eating springrolls. Springrolls are fried rice tubes filled with pork, noodles, shrimp, and mushrooms.

Durian (DYOO-ree-uhn) is a Vietnamese fruit. It is round and green. Vietnamese people eat the soft insides of durians. Durians have an awful smell but taste sweet.

Pho is a popular food in Vietnam.

Animals in Vietnam

Tigers, deer, and crocodiles live in Vietnam. Leopards and black bears wander through the mountains. Poisonous snakes like the king cobra slide through the jungles.

Vietnam is home to the giant muntjac. This deer-like animal barks like a dog. It has large teeth in the back of its mouth.

In 1992, scientists discovered a new kind of ox in Vietnam. They named it the Vu Quang (VOO KWAHNG) ox. This is because scientists found the ox in Vu Quang forest. The Vu Quang ox looks like a deer. It has straight, sharp horns.

The Javan rhinoceros lives in Vietnam. It is one of the rarest animals in the world. The Javan rhinoceros has one horn. It weighs up to 3,300 pounds (1,485 kilograms).

People use animals to help them farm. The water buffalo is a common work animal.

Water buffalo is a common work animal.

Homes and Clothing

Many Vietnamese people live in villages. They build houses out of bamboo. They make roofs out of palm leaves or straw. Other Vietnamese people live in boats on rivers. In cities, families live in small houses or apartments.

Many men wear loose tunics called ao the (OW THAIR). Tunics are long shirts with long sleeves. The tunics have slits on the sides. The slits allow legs to move freely. Women wear tunics called ao dai (OW ZAI). Both men and women wear black pants or white pants.

Many Vietnamese people do not wear shoes. Some wear wooden sandals called guoc (GWOK). Guoc have thick high heels. They help people keep their clothes out of the mud.

Vietnamese women sometimes wear pointed hats called non la (NOHN LAH). These hats keep the sun off their faces.

Some Vietnamese people live in boats on rivers.

Vietnamese Sports

Soccer is the most popular sport in Vietnam. Swimming is another favorite sport. Vietnamese people also enjoy badminton, handball, volleyball, and table tennis. Some Vietnamese people play golf.

Vietnamese people want to be active and healthy. Children learn to jump, skip, and somersault. Schools require all students to practice gymnastics. Gymnastics are exercises that use controlled body movements.

Many Vietnamese people learn thai cuc quyen (THAI KUK KYEN). Thai cuc quyen is a pattern of slow gymnastic exercises. People who live in cities practice thai cuc quyen together. They practice in parks and on street corners.

Other Vietnamese people learn martial arts. A martial art is a way of defending oneself or fighting.

Some Vietnamese people learn martial arts.

Holidays

The most important holiday in Vietnam is Tet. Tet is the Vietnamese New Year. People celebrate Tet in late January or early February. People celebrate Tet for at least three days. Some people celebrate it even longer.

Parents do not work during Tet. Children stay home from school for a week. People decorate their houses with plum flowers. Family members and friends gather to celebrate together.

Wandering Soul's Day is an important holiday in August. People say special prayers at pagodas. A pagoda is a temple. People leave food and presents in graveyards. These are gifts for the spirits of forgotten dead people.

May 19 is Ho Chi Minh's (HOH CHEE MING) Birthday. People consider Ho Chi Minh the father of modern Vietnam. He helped free Vietnam from French rule.

People say special prayers at pagodas on holidays.

Hands On: Bite the Carp's Tail

The carp is a popular fish in Vietnam. Some Vietnamese people believe the carp brings good luck. Vietnamese children enjoy playing bite the carp's tail.

What You Need
Six or more players
A large playing area

What You Do
1. Choose a leader for the game. The other players should line up behind that person. They should put their hands on the shoulders of the person in front of them.
2. The first person is the carp's head. The last person in line is the carp's tail.
3. Everyone should run when the leader says go. The line must not break. Each person must hold on to the person in front. The head leads the line. The head tries to catch the tail. The tail tries to run away from the head. If the head tags the tail, the head earns a point.
4. If the line breaks, the carp dies. Then the head moves to the back of the line. The head becomes the tail. The next person in line becomes the new head.
5. The player with the most points wins.

Learn to Speak Vietnamese

good night	chuc ngu ngon	(CHOOK NGOO NGON)
hello	xin chao	(SIN CHOW)
my name is	ten toi la	(TAIN TOY LAH)
no	khong	(kah-OHNG)
please	lam on	(LAHM UHN)
thank you	cam on	(KAHM UHN)
yes (north)	vang	(vah-UHNG)
yes (south)	da	(YAH)

Words to Know

delta (DEL-tuh)—a wide, wet area that is good for crops

durian (DYOO-ree-uhn)—a Vietnamese fruit

pagoda (pah-GOH-dah)—a temple

pho (FUH)—thick noodle and beef soup

thai cuc quyen (THAI KUK KYEN)—a pattern of slow gymnastic exercises

tunic (TOO-nik)—a long shirt with long sleeves

xoi (SOY)—sticky rice mixed with peanuts or beans and wrapped in a leaf

Read More

Kalman, Bobbi. *Vietnam, the People*. New York: Crabtree Publishing Company, 1996.

O'Connor, Karen. *Vietnam*. Globe-Trotters Club. Minneapolis: Carolrhoda Books, 1999.

Useful Addresses and Internet Sites

Liaison Office of the Socialist Republic of Vietnam
1233 20th Street NW
Washington, DC 20036

State of the World's Children
UNICEF
1 UN Plaza
New York, NY 10017

Destination: Vietnam Kids
http://www.destinationvietnam.com/kids/kids.htm

Vietnam Pictures Archive at Sunsite
http://sunsite.unc.edu/vietnam/

Index